Robert
PATTINSON

Tamra Orr

Mitchell Lane
PUBLISHERS
P.O. Box 196
Hockessin, Delaware 19707
Visit us on the web: www.mitchelllane.com
Comments? email us: mitchelllane@mitchelllane.com

Printing   1   2   3   4   5   6   7   8   9

Blue Banner Biographies

Akon	Flo Rida	Megan Fox
Alicia Keys	Gwen Stefani	Miguel Tejada
Allen Iverson	Ice Cube	Missy Elliott
Ashanti	Ja Rule	Nancy Pelosi
Ashlee Simpson	Jamie Foxx	Natasha Bedingfield
Ashton Kutcher	Jay-Z	Orianthi
Avril Lavigne	Jennifer Lopez	Orlando Bloom
Beyoncé	Jessica Simpson	P. Diddy
Blake Lively	J. K. Rowling	Peyton Manning
Bow Wow	Joe Flacco	Pink
Brett Favre	John Legend	Queen Latifah
Britney Spears	Johnny Depp	Rihanna
Carrie Underwood	Justin Berfield	**Robert Pattinson**
Chris Brown	Justin Timberlake	Ron Howard
Chris Daughtry	Kanye West	Sean Kingston
Christina Aguilera	Kate Hudson	Selena
Christopher Paul Curtis	Keith Urban	Shakira
Ciara	Kelly Clarkson	Shia LaBeouf
Clay Aiken	Kenny Chesney	Shontelle Layne
Cole Hamels	Kristen Stewart	Soulja Boy Tell 'Em
Condoleezza Rice	Lady Gaga	Stephenie Meyer
Corbin Bleu	Lance Armstrong	Taylor Swift
Daniel Radcliffe	Leona Lewis	T.I.
David Ortiz	Lil Wayne	Timbaland
David Wright	Lindsay Lohan	Tim McGraw
Derek Jeter	Mariah Carey	Toby Keith
Drew Brees	Mario	Usher
Eminem	Mary J. Blige	Vanessa Anne Hudgens
Eve	Mary-Kate and Ashley Olsen	Zac Efron
Fergie (Stacy Ferguson)		

Library of Congress Cataloging-in-Publication Data
Orr, Tamra.
  Robert Pattinson / by Tamra Orr.
    p. cm. — (Blue banner biographies)
  Includes bibliographical references and index.
  ISBN 978-1-58415-905-6 (library bound)
  1. Pattinson, Robert, 1986– —Juvenile literature. 2. Motion picture actors and actresses—Juvenile literature.—Great Britain—Biography I. Title.
  PN2598.P36O77 2011
  792.0'28092—dc22
  [B]
                                                                    2010006564

ABOUT THE AUTHOR: Tamra Orr is the author of more than 250 nonfiction books for readers of all ages, including *Kristen Stewart* in the Blue Banner Biography series and more than two dozen other celebrity biographies. Several of her books have won awards, including the New York Public Library Best Nonfiction Book for Teens and Youth Advocates Honorable Mention. Orr lives in the Pacific Northwest with her children, husband, cat, and dog, and in her spare time she reads and watches movies starring the people she just wrote about.

PUBLISHER'S NOTE: The following story has been thoroughly researched, and to the best of our knowledge represents a true story. While every possible effort has been made to ensure accuracy, the publisher will not assume liability for damages caused by inaccuracies in the data and makes no warranty on the accuracy of the information contained herein. This story has not been authorized or endorsed by Robert Pattinson.

Everywhere Robert Pattinson goes, adoring fans are sure to follow.
Hundreds of them line up to get the star's autograph.

An Unexpected Beginning

*I*t was just supposed to be a quick dinner at a local restaurant, but it turned out to be a life-changing stop. Young Robert and his father were chatting and they happened to spot a few young ladies at another table. They seemed excited about something—and Pattinson asked what it was. They had just come from the Barnes Theatre Club, a London acting group. Today, Pattinson says, "I owe everything to the Barnes Theatre Club. I wouldn't be acting if it wasn't for that little club." It was in this small club that he got his start—and ended up becoming one of the hottest, most recognized stars in the world.

After listening to the girls talk about the acting club, Mr. Pattinson decided that this might be a good avenue for his son. Young Pattinson recalls, "I only did it [acting] because my dad saw a bunch of pretty girls in a restaurant and he asked them where they came from and they said drama group. He said, 'Son, that is where you need to go.'" The concept of becoming an actor was new to the boy. "I thought drama was stupid but I think my dad had some kind of weird foresight," he admits. As time passed by, his father "nagged me about attending. At one point, he said he would pay me,

A very young Pattinson would dash away from his mother when they played at the park — so she would put him in a harness to keep him safe.

which is pretty strange—I don't know what his intentions were, but I went."

From a very young age, Robert Pattinson showed an ability to act. Even in prep school, teachers remarked on how well he did on stage—although he did not do nearly as well in class. He was often in trouble for not finishing his homework. In fact, although this boy would eventually win many different awards for his acting ability, his first official award was a much lesser known one: the most untidy desk award! Fortunately, a sloppy desk was not enough to hold him back from becoming one of the world's biggest stars.

CHAPTER 2

The Pattinson Family

*T*oday, the face of Robert Pattinson can be seen practically everywhere. His smile flashes on movie and television screens. His tousled hair graces the covers of books. His blue eyes light up photographs for magazine and newspaper interviews. It is hard to believe that just a few years ago, few people had ever heard of this young Brit. Where did this young adult who has portrayed everything from a handsome Triwizard champion to an immortal 107-year-old vampire come from?

Robert Thomas Pattinson was born on May 13, 1986, in London, England. His father, Robert, was an importer of American cars. According to the younger Pattinson, "My dad is from Yorkshire and he did a bunch of things. In the seventies, he moved to America for a bit and just worked as a taxi driver. Then he started selling cars in the eighties." Clare, his mother, worked for a modeling agency based in London. Now, both are retired.

When Robert was born, he joined his five-year-old sister Victoria and three-year-old sister Elizabeth, or Lizzy. The two girls loved having a little brother to play with—and dress up.

For Pattinson's two sisters, the young heartthrob was a favorite toy that they could dress up and use in their games.

"Up until I was twelve, my sisters used to dress me up as a girl and introduce me as Claudia," recalls Pattinson.

At age six, Robert went to Tower House, a private school in East Sheen in southwest London. It was there that he was given his first role: the King of Hearts in the school's *Spell for a Rhyme*. Next, he played Robert in *Lord of the Flies*. At twelve, he began attending Harrodian School and the Barnes Theatre Club. His life began to change in many ways. Along with having his own paper route, he "was obsessed with earning money until I was about fifteen." Already able to play the piano since the age of three, he also taught himself how to play guitar at the age of five. He even became part of a band, which he described as "pretty hardcore for three private school kids from suburban London. And my mum's like, cramping our style, popping her head in to ask, 'You boys want a sandwich?' "

Along with acting, playing music, and going to school, Robert also began doing some modeling, thanks to a connection his mother had through the agency where she worked. "I was modeling at twelve, the youngest person in my agency out of the girls or boys," he describes. "I was so ridiculously skinny I looked like a girl, but that was the period where they loved androgynous-looking people." He did a number of clothing ads, plus some for jewelry companies. It did not last long, however, because his passion for acting took over. His sister Lizzy had already done some acting and dancing. At age seventeen, she was spotted by an agent who hired her to join the dance band Aurora. With the group, she had two songs hit the U.K. Top 20 ("Dreaming" and "The Day It Rained Forever") and a #1 Billboard Dance Chart Hit ("Let the Sunshine In").

> *"Up until I was twelve, my sisters used to dress me up as a girl and introduce me as Claudia."*

At Barnes, Robert started off behind the scenes. He helped build sets and worked on the technical aspects of putting on a play. Finally, however, he decided to try out for a role. "I auditioned for *Guys and Dolls* and got a little tiny part as some Cuban dancer or something," he recalls, ". . . and then in the next play, I got the lead part." He performed in *Macbeth*, *Anything Goes* and *Tess of the D'Urbervilles*. It was in his role as Alec d'Urberville that Pattinson was spotted by a talent agent — and his life took a magical turn that he could never have predicted.

As Cedric Diggory in Harry Potter and the Goblet of Fire, *Pattinson played an athlete—and a hero.*

CHAPTER 3

Becoming Part of Hogwarts

Now that Pattinson had an agent, the opportunities to act increased. His first cinematic role, as Reese Witherspoon's son in *Vanity Fair*, ended up on the cutting-room floor. (His deleted scenes are on the director's cut of the DVD, however.) His second role was a character named Giselher in a television movie. In Germany it was called *Ring of the Nibelungs*, but in the United States it aired as *Dark Kingdom: The Dragon King*.

In between filming these two movies, Pattinson was sent on an audition for the role that would catapult him into theaters across the planet in *Harry Potter and the Goblet of Fire*. He read for the part of the extremely handsome Cedric Diggory, a sixth-year Hufflepuff student. "Cedric exemplifies all that you would expect the Hogwarts champion to be," explains Mike Newell, director of the film. "Robert Pattinson was born to play the role; he's quintessentially English with chiseled public schoolboy good looks."

Pattinson got the role — and received wonderful reviews for it. *The London Evening Standard* wrote that his portrayal of Diggory was superb. "He is one of the bright new stars of the latest Harry Potter film," stated the critic. "Now Robert Pattinson is being dubbed 'the next Jude Law' for a screen-stealing performance as the dashing head boy in 'Harry Potter and the Goblet of Fire'. The London-born teenager, who plays Potter's love rival, will set hearts racing among female cinema-goers when the film is released . . ."

Indeed, that is just what happened. Young teens throughout the U.S. and U.K. were already huge fans of Daniel Radcliffe (Harry Potter), Emma Watson (Hermione Granger), and Rupert Grint (Ron Weasley), and now they had a new character to adore. Pattinson joined his cast mates for photo shoots and parties.

> *Being part of the film was exhausting and dangerous, calling on physical abilities Pattinson was not sure he had.*

Being part of the film was exhausting and dangerous, calling on physical abilities Pattinson was not sure he had. For example, in one part of the movie, several of the characters, including Cedric, had to swim through Black Lake in order to rescue people they cared about as part of the Triwizard competition. The problem was that Pattinson barely knew how to swim, let alone spend time underwater rescuing his onscreen girlfriend, Cho Chang (Katie Leung).

At first, the characters practiced their moves in a small tank—but then they had to move to a much bigger one in order to simulate an entire lake. "I had never done scuba diving before," Pattinson explains. "I was in a tiny little tub that was a practice tank. I didn't see the big tank until they first started shooting in it. It was about a hundred times the size of the practice tank and it was so much deeper, so that was sort of scary when I first got there, because you have to get used to all the pressure and things like that."

The cast from the fourth Harry Potter movie spent a lot of time getting to know each other on and off the set.

It took skill to look like he knew what he was doing—and keep acting. Breathing was an issue, also, as his character was supposed to look like he had a Bubble-Head Charm that would allow him to breathe underwater. "It is completely blue in there and there are divers with breathing equipment that are completely blue as well," describes Pattinson. "You can't really see anything. You just get this breather put into your mouth after the take has been done. I got used to it quickly though."

Along with learning how to swim well, Pattinson had to endure the maze—almost as frightening in real life to work in as it appeared in the movie. "In the maze, a lot of it was on steady cam—which is just a guy running around with a

Emma, Katie, and Robert promoted their movie all around the world. They even attended a premiere in Japan with director Mike Newell (right).

camera—and all the hedges moved," says Pattinson. "So me and Dan were basically chasing each other around and punching each other, with these hedges squeezing us. It was so real. And because it was all hydraulic walls, no one actually knew if it would kill you or not, if you actually got trapped there."

Cedric Diggory has a final run-in with Wormtail and the Avada Kedavra spell. It is a turning point in the film series, as it becomes darker and more sinister. Pattinson's portrayal of a handsome, promising head boy being struck down so young was one that impressed moviegoers—and film directors—alike.

CHAPTER 4

Being Independent

When Pattinson finished filming *Harry Potter and the Goblet of Fire*, he was ready to take some time off. He had made quite a bit of money for this part, so he took a year to play music and hang out with his friends. Getting used to the worldwide attention of the media — and thousands of screaming fans — was difficult for him. "The day before [the *Harry Potter* London premiere] I was just sitting in Leicester Square, happily being ignored by everyone," he says. "Then suddenly strangers are screaming your name. Amazing."

Pattinson was offered several roles after *Potter*. In 2006, he starred in a movie called *The Haunted Airman*. In it, he plays a World War II veteran named Toby Jugg. A supernatural thriller, it revolves around Jugg, who is paralyzed and kept in a wheelchair in a mysterious and threatening hospital.

Following this, Pattinson played Daniel Gale in a television movie called *The Bad Mother's Handbook*. Gale is a young man who falls in love with his teacher, a struggling single mother. Next, Pattinson put in a brief appearance in *Harry Potter and the Order of the Phoenix*, and then starred in three small, independent films: *The Summer House*, *How to Be*, and *Little Ashes*.

Despite his fame, Pattinson still enjoys spending time with his longtime friends and fellow English actors Tom Sturridge (left) and Andrew Garfield (center).

In The Haunted Airman, *Pattinson has a brush with the supernatural — good preparation for the film role still waiting in the wings.*

In *Little Ashes*, Pattinson had the chance, for the first time, to play an actual person: artist Salvador Dalí. In an interview with *The London Evening Standard*, he said, "Playing Dalí has been a complete turning point for me. It's the first part I've had that has required really serious thought. I became completely obsessed with Dalí during the filming, and I read every biography I could get hold of."

Pattinson's good looks have helped make him a star, but it is talent in front of the camera that has brought him to where he is today. He had to transform himself into the eccentric artist Dalí, and make his character believable.

Because most of the cast spoke Spanish and Pattinson did not, he spent a great deal of time alone. "I just read and read and read, and it was one of the most satisfying jobs I've ever done because it was the one time that I really had zero distractions," he admits. "It really changed my whole attitude toward acting. And it was a tiny, tiny film, which I don't think anyone will ever see, probably! But it was very interesting. Especially since I don't look anything like Dalí. But at the end of the job, I kind of did look like him."

Although Pattinson was in several films, his career was not taking off like he had hoped. Finally, he came to a decision. It was time to pursue a different profession. His dad was wrong—acting was not the way to go. He had one more audition set up for some movie called *Twilight*, but he knew he was up against thousands of other young, handsome, talented actors. He suspected he had little chance of getting the role. This time, Pattinson could not have been more wrong.

> **Because most of the cast spoke Spanish and Pattinson did not, he spent a great deal of time alone.**

Everything about Pattinson's dark, brooding looks was perfect for the role of the vampire Edward Cullen.

Twilight and Beyond

When he appeared at the audition for the role of Edward Cullen in the new film series *Twilight*, Pattinson was about ready to call it quits. "I was literally, the day before I did this audition; I was going to quit acting. I was going to quit because I never got any jobs," he said, "so I guess it's not really quitting when you're not getting jobs—it's just surrendering to fate." Fortunately, he changed his mind. Millions of young readers throughout the world had already read the bestselling *Twilight* series. When it was announced that the first book would be turned into a movie, fans were thrilled. They were curious too—who would play the beloved roles of Bella and Edward? They did not have long to wait.

Pattinson's audition for Edward took place at director Catherine Hardwicke's home. "I'd seen a zillion really cute guys," she recalls. "But that was the problem. They all looked like the super-cute kid in your high school. The prom king, or the captain of the football team. They didn't look like they were from another world and time."

Actress Kristen Stewart, who had been cast as Bella, agreed with Hardwicke. "Everybody came in doing something empty and shallow and thoughtless—but Rob

Kristen Stewart wanted Pattinson to play Edward from his first audition. The two became close friends off the set as they played sweethearts in Twilight.

understood that it wasn't a frivolous role," she said. "Not to put down any of the other actors who came in, because they were really good, but everyone came in playing Edward as this perfect, happy-go-lucky guy, but I got hardcore pain from Rob. It was purely just connection."

Pattinson's performance thrilled and surprised Hardwicke, Stewart, and everyone else. It even surprised Pattinson. "I went in having no idea how to play the part at all and thinking there was no chance of getting it," he admits. " I mean, Catherine literally didn't say anything during the whole audition. She just filmed. And Kristen did it so differently to how I was expecting Bella to be played that it kind of shocked a performance out of me."

> "Everybody came in doing something empty and shallow and thoughtless— but Rob understood that it wasn't a frivolous role."

Not everyone was happy with the choice, however. Angry fans felt Pattinson was not right for the role of Edward, and 75,000 of them signed a petition asking Hardwicke to change her mind and get someone else. This time, author Stephenie Meyer stepped up to defend the choice. "The one guy that kids were always saying they wanted for Edward was Tom Welling from *Smallville*," she explained. "He's beautiful! But could you ever imagine being afraid of him? We did not have a good option until Rob came along. And the movie rests entirely on his shoulders. I am ecstatic with Summit's choice for Edward. There are very few actors who can look both dangerous and beautiful at the same time, and even fewer who I can picture in my head as Edward. Robert Pattinson is going to be amazing."

Filming *Twilight* and a then its sequel, *New Moon*, was quite an experience for Pattinson. It was hard work physically. Although he did quite a few of the stunts, he quickly learned that stunt doubles exist for a reason. "I had a good stunt double. . . . He's a professional free runner. I can do something and get injured and look like crap playing it or he can do it and make it look really good and no one notices the difference," he admits. "After a while, I tried to do the Tom Cruise thing, but I eventually gave up. But I did a whole bunch of it. I managed to pick up so many injuries whenever I tried the simplest of stunts. I went to pick up Kristen and I almost ripped my hamstring. It's not even a stunt. I literally did one squat. And this was after three months of training."

> **After the first movie came out, Pattinson's life changed radically. Everywhere he went, girls would scream and cry.**

After the first movie came out, Pattinson's life changed radically. Everywhere he went, girls would scream and cry. Many lined up for hours just for a glimpse of him. He was invited on talk shows, entertainment shows, and radio shows. It was not easy for the usually quiet and shy Pattinson to get used to. "Everything has become more intense for six months, since *Twilight* was released," he says. "It's hard to handle what's happening to me. I don't have the necessary hindsight, even if only to find a way out to this situation. But this celebrity thing, you can't fight it, it's useless, you can't avoid it. When it's not something you desired during your whole life, or something you don't aspire to, you're free not to care about it." He continued, saying, "I don't know why it still shocks me. I

When you are as famous as Pattinson, it is hard to go out without getting mobbed by fans. He often tries to disguise himself with sunglasses and hats to escape the cameras.

mean, I've been going for the last three weeks, just going to different cities all around the world, just to get to these planned mobbings, where everybody just screams and screams and screams. But every single time, I get so nervous and have cold sweats, and everything."

The third movie of the series, *Eclipse*, was scheduled for release in mid-2010, and the fourth, *Breaking Dawn*, in 2011. For all four films, Pattinson would earn millions of dollars — and millions of adoring fans. With all of that accomplished by such a young age, what would the future hold?

Pattinson has used his musical talents in several movies. In How to Be, he played guitar and sang. He also played "Bella's Lullaby" on the piano in Twilight.

A Bright Future

Most likely, Robert Pattinson will continue to act even after the *Twilight* movies come to an end. In just a few years, he has managed to win numerous awards, including four Teen Choice awards, two People's Choice awards, three MTV awards, and one from the Hollywood Film Festival. Despite all of these, he keeps other possible careers in mind as well. "Music is my backup plan if acting fails," Pattinson told the *Los Angeles Times*. "I don't want to put all of my eggs in one basket."

Music is certainly one of the star's talents, from writing to singing and playing. Two of his original songs appear on the *Twilight* soundtrack: "Never Think" and "Let Me Sign." He has been involved with music for a long time, although it has taken a backseat during his movie days. "A lot of my friends are actors and we have so little to do all the time, so instead of just being bored, we were like, 'Why not start a band?' " he says. "So we did. . . . I still try and play, but it's weird now since when I am trying to do it as an actor, it always seems kind of cheesy. I liked playing at open mics in bars and stuff because it was the only time I really felt free. I did a couple of

Pattinson has earned a number of awards already in his brief acting career, including three awards from MTV.

gigs in L.A. . . . I'm going to wait for all this to die down before I start doing live gigs again."

In addition to movies and music, Pattinson has been involved in several charities. In 2009, he auctioned off two kisses (on the cheek) for over $20,000 to raise money for the American Foundation for AIDS Research. In early 2010, he also appeared on Hope for Haiti Now: A Global Benefit for Earthquake Relief, along with stars such as Brad Pitt, Madonna, and Beyoncé.

Naturally, as a single handsome celebrity, much of the stories written about Pattinson wonder about whom he is dating. He has been paired off in stories with costars from Emma Watson to Kristen Stewart. What does Pattinson say about it? Not much. Instead, he just tells his fans, "My dog is the only lady friend in my life. I have a really girly dog but she hasn't got a girly attitude."

It is unlikely that his dog will remain the only lady in Pattinson's life. In the meantime, he will keep thrilling and entertaining fans across the world. Whether as a wizard, vampire, or something entirely different in between, he is sure to amaze his audiences, young and old.

In 2009, [Robert] auctioned off two kisses (on the cheek) for over $20,000 to raise money for the American Foundation for AIDS Research.

CHRONOLOGY

1986	Robert Thomas Pattinson is born in London on May 13
1992	Begins attending Tower House School
1998	Begins attending Harrodian School and joins Barnes Theatre Club
2004	Lands his first movie roles
2005	Is cast as Cedric Diggory in *Harry Potter and the Goblet of Fire*
2006	Stars in *The Haunted Airman*
2008	Appears in several independent films; stars in *Twilight*
2009	Wins multiple awards; stars in *New Moon*
2010	Stars in *Eclipse*

FILMOGRAPHY

2010	*Remember Me*
	The Twilight Saga: Eclipse
	Unbound Captives
2009	*The Twilight Saga: New Moon*
2008	*The Summer House*
	How to Be
	Little Ashes
	Twilight
2007	*The Bad Mother's Handbook* (TV)
	Harry Potter and the Order of the Phoenix
2006	*The Haunted Airman* (TV)
2005	*Harry Potter and the Goblet of Fire*
2004	*Vanity Fair*
	Ring of the Nibelungs (Dark Kingdom: The Dragon King) (TV)

FURTHER READING

Books

Adams, Isabelle. *Robert Pattinson: Eternally Yours*. New York: HarperCollins, 2008.

Besel, Jennifer. *Robert Pattinson*. Bel Air, CA: Snap Books, 2009.

Harte, Harlee. *I (Heart) Robert Pattinson*. Beverly Hills, CA: Dove Books, 2009.

Rusher, Josie. *Robert Pattinson: True Love Never Dies*. Toronto: Orion, 2009.

Stenning, Paul. *The Robert Pattinson Album*. London, England: Plexus Publishing, 2009.

Tieck, Sarah. *Robert Pattinson*. Edina, MN: Abdo Publishing Co., 2010.

Williams, Mel. *Robert Pattinson: Fated for Fame*. New York: Simon Pulse, 2009.

Works Consulted

Celebrity Central: Robert Pattinson. *People.com*
http://www.people.com/people/robert_pattinson

Finburg, Kate. "Star of Vampire Movie Twilight Owes His Success to Barncs Theatre Club." *Croydon Guardian*, December 5, 2008.

Inbar, Michael. "Robert Pattinson Talks about Dating Kristen." *MSNBC.com*, November 19, 2009. http://today.msnbc.msn.com/id/34037192/ns/today-today_entertainment/

Maloney, Alison. "Hunk Was 'Girl Called Claudia.'" *The Sun.co.uk*, January 2, 2009. http://www.thesun.co.uk/sol/homepage/showbiz/film/article2089064.ece

Morreale, Marie. "Robert Pattinson as Cedric Diggory in *Harry Potter and the Goblet of Fire*." *Scholastic News*. http://teacher.scholastic.com/scholasticnews/indepth/harry_potter_movic_iv/interviews/index.asp?article=pattinson&topic=1

Neill, Beth. "Twilight Exclusive — Robert Pattinson: I Haven't Got a Girlfriend." *Mirror.co.uk*. August 19, 2009. http://www.mirror.co.uk/celebs/news/2009/08/19/twighlight-exclusive-robert-pattinson-i-haven-t-got-a-girlfriend-115875-21606942/

On the Internet

Official Movie Site for *Twilight* Films
http://www.twilightthemovie.com/

Robert Pattinson Fan Club
http://robertpattinson.org/

ROBsessed
http://www.robsessedpattinson.com/